Protecting Habitats

PROTECTING
Temperate
Forests

Moira Butterfield

GARETH**STEVENS**
GS
PUBLISHING
A Member of the WRC Media Family of Companies

Please visit our web site at: www.garethstevens.com
For a free color catalog describing Gareth Stevens Publishing's list of high-quality books
and multimedia programs, call 1-800-542-2595 (USA) or 1-800-387-3178 (Canada).
Gareth Stevens Publishing's fax: (414) 332-3567.

Library of Congress Cataloging-in-Publication Data

Butterfield, Moira, 1961-
    Protecting temperate forests / by Moira Butterfield. — North American ed.
    p. cm. — (Protecting habitats)
    Includes index.
    ISBN 0-8368-4995-7 (lib. bdg.)
    1. Forests and forestry—Juvenile literature. 2. Habitat conservation—Juvenile
literature. 1. Title. II. Series.
    QH86.B882   2005
    577.3—dc22   2005042627

This North American edition first published in 2006 by
Gareth Stevens Publishing
A Member of the WRC Media Family of Companies
330 West Olive Street, Suite 100
Milwaukee, WI 53212 USA

This U.S. edition copyright © 2006 by Gareth Stevens, Inc. Original edition copyright © 2004 by Franklin Watts.
First published in Great Britain in 2004 by Franklin Watts, 96 Leonard Street, London, EC2A 4XD, UK.

Designer: Rita Storey
Editor: Sarah Ridley
Art Director: Jonathan Hair
Editor-in-Chief: John C. Miles
Picture Research: Susan Mennell
Map and graph artwork: Ian Thompson

Gareth Stevens Editor: Gini Holland
Gareth Stevens Cover Design: Dave Kowalski

Photo Credits: Cover images: Ecoscene, Ecoscene: pp. 1, 4, 7, 8-9, 10, 11, 12, 16, 19, 20, 21, 22, 23, 24, 25, 26
Oxford Scientific Films: pp. 15, 27

Printed in the United States of America

1 2 3 4 5 6 7 8 9 09 08 07 06 05

CONTENTS

All about Forests

The densely packed trees of this English woodland create a magical atmosphere in late spring as light filters through the green canopy.

Forests cover a vast area of our planet's surface. This huge environment is thought to have a significant effect on Earth's weather, temperature, and even the air we breathe.

Defining Woodlands and Forests

Earth can be divided by an imaginary line, called the equator, around its center. Above and below the equator lie the Northern and Southern Hemispheres.

The more southern part of the Northern Hemisphere is home to woodlands, made up mainly of deciduous trees, which lose their leaves in winter. Further north is the huge boreal forest, made up mainly of evergreen trees, which keep their leaves the whole year round.

Many areas of Earth near the equator are wrapped in lush, green, tropical rain forests, which are not discussed in this book. Areas of cooler, temperate rain forests also thrive, however, in both the Northern and Southern Hemispheres.

Standing among the Trees

If you visited a woodland, you would find a mixture of trees, such as maple, beech, and birch. Many of them are broad-leaved trees. You might see birds and small mammals busy looking for food. On the ground, you would find flowers growing on the forest floor. In winter, the trees would be bare, standing over a carpet of fallen leaves.

The boreal forest stretches around the world, through North America, Europe, Scandinavia, and Asia. Two-thirds of it grows in Russia, where it is called the taiga. In total, it covers 6.4 million square miles (16.6 million square kilometers), making it the largest land biome on Earth. The boreal forest has trees such as firs, spruce, and conifers. Here you find less wildlife and fewer small plants.

If you stood in a temperate rain forest, you would be surrounded by a small number of tree types, with some growing to a huge size. On the ground, you would see mosses, ferns, and other moisture-loving plants. The air would feel cool and wet most of the time.

BIOME UNDER THREAT

Forests have grown on Earth for hundreds of millions of years, and for centuries, humans have cut them down for timber or to clear the land for farming. In modern times, cutting has speeded up, threatening forest renewal. Another modern threat is industrial pollution, which has brought deadly acid rain to the forests, killing trees and poisoning the soil. Loss of large forest areas is called deforestation. In this book, you can find out what is being done to control deforestation and how scientists are trying to battle pollution and predict what effects tree loss may have on the world. You can also find out what you can do yourself to help preserve Earth's forests.

Different Kinds of Forests

The farther north you go in the Northern Hemisphere, the colder it is and the shorter the summers are. Areas near the coasts get extra rainfall and fog. These variations in climate affect the types of trees that will grow in each area.

Woodlands

Woodlands are found in the southern part of the Northern Hemisphere because the climate is moderate, and it rains regularly through the year. Here, the deciduous trees have a growing season of between 140 and 200 days when it is warm enough for them to make the energy they need to grow.

As winter approaches, the trees store the nutrients from their leaves to use as an energy supply during the winter. The drying leaves die and fall to the ground.

As the dead leaves gradually rot, the quality of the soil is improved, which makes the deciduous forest floor a good place for small plants and fungi to grow.

There are several different types of woodlands. Some woodlands have a mixture of broad-leaved and needle-leaved trees growing together in the same forest.

The Boreal Forest

The boreal forest is named after Boreas, the ancient Greek god of the chilly north wind. In boreal forest areas, summers are short and wet. Winters are long, severely cold, and dry, and the ground freezes. The trees have only a short, 130-day growing season.

Winters are colder the further north you go in the boreal forest. Winter temperatures can plunge as low as -65° Fahrenheit

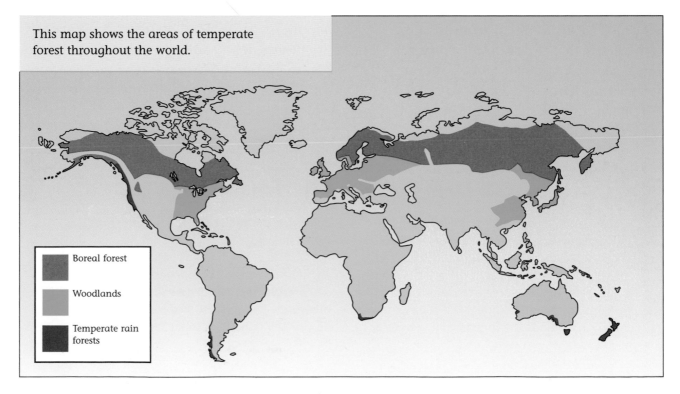

This map shows the areas of temperate forest throughout the world.

Boreal forest

Woodlands

Temperate rain forests

(-54° Celsius), which is too cold for most creatures to survive. The soil here is poor, so, compared to woodlands, there are few small plants growing on the forest floor.

In the United States, the boreal forest stretches from Alaska to the Great Lakes, and isolated stretches grow on some high mountains, such as the Appalachians.

Temperate Rain Forests

Most of the world's rain forests grow in the hot climate around the equator. Along the Pacific northwest coast of the United States, however, the weather is mild and wet enough for temperate rain forests to grow. The trees here are ancient and rare and include Sitka spruces which live for over one thousand years. The Southern Hemisphere also supports areas of temperate rain forests in Australia, New Zealand, South Africa, and Chile.

Unlike the trees in the boreal forest, evergreens can grow all year round in the rain forest because of the mild climate. These conditions allow some species to grow to a huge size. Epiphytes, which are plants that grow on other plants, also thrive here. They hang down from the tree branches and dangle their roots in the air to get the moisture they need. The temperate rain forest areas of Australia and New Zealand contain tree and animal species found nowhere else.

Giant redwood trees in the Pacific coast forests of the United States can reach heights of 300 feet (90 meters) and up to 100 feet (30 m) around.

How Trees Work

Trees do things in processes that affect our climate, the land we live on, and the air we breathe. Because the northern forests and woodlands are so huge, these processes have a marked effect that scientists can measure.

Photosynthesis

Trees create their own food by a process called photosynthesis. They take in water and a gas called carbon dioxide (CO_2). Then, using sunlight and a green chemical called chlorophyll, the leaves convert the water and CO_2 into sugar and oxygen (O_2). The sugar is used as fuel to help the tree grow. The oxygen is expelled into the air.

During the growing season of the huge northern forest regions, there is so much photosynthesis going on that scientists can measure worldwide levels of CO_2 falling — and levels of oxygen rising. If northern forests disappear, that high level of photosynthesis will drop. That drop could have a drastic effect on Earth's air and climate.

Carbon dioxide is a gas that is released when fuel, such as wood or coal, burns. Too much carbon dioxide in the air leads to global warming — when Earth's climate gets warmer (*see page 18*). Oxygen is a gas that all life on Earth needs in order to survive. With less photosynthesis, we would have more CO_2 and less O_2 in the atmosphere.

Water Recycling

Trees are champion water recyclers. When water falls to the ground as rain or snow, trees take up the water through their roots. This water eventually gets recycled back into the air when it evaporates out through the leaves. Finally, it falls to Earth again, and the process repeats itself.

If huge areas of forest disappear, this natural water recycling will decline, and there could be an effect on the amount of rain that falls around the world. Farming might suffer, affecting our food supplies.

Soil Anchors

Tree roots help anchor the topsoil to the ground. Holding topsoil in place is especially important in the boreal forest, where the soil is thin and sandy. If the boreal forest is destroyed, this poor, thin soil will not be good for farming, and the wind will easily blow it away.

We can find an example of what might happen by looking back in history. In the 1930s, large-scale tree cutting and farmers plowing up the prairies helped cause a "dust bowl" in the midwestern United States, making life there very difficult. Terrible dust storms occurred, caused as the wind blew the soil away.

The Secret of Leaves

Water is the key to why deciduous trees lose their leaves and why evergreen trees keep their needles. When cold weather comes to the Northern Hemisphere, the ground freezes. Frozen water is impossible for trees to collect

through their roots. Instead, they need to save a store of water inside them while they wait for spring to come.

Broad leaves lose water quickly because water evaporates out of their wide surfaces. In winter, losing so much moisture would mean death for a broad-leaved tree, so it is better for the leaves to die off and then regrow in spring when the ground thaws.

Needle-shaped leaves do not lose anywhere near as much water because their surfaces are very small and they have a waxy coating on them. Therefore, they do not need to die off in winter, and as soon as the sun comes out in spring, they can start photosynthesizing again. This way, evergreen trees get the longest possible growing season where summers are short.

The leaves of deciduous trees turn beautiful colors before they die and fall off in autumn.

The Life of a Tree

Fallen "nurse logs" in a temperate rain forest provide good places for tree seedlings to grow.

Many different types of trees grow in woodlands and forests around the world, but they all have some things in common. They grow leaves (or needles), seeds, and new wood.

Trees from Seeds

A tree begins its life by sprouting from a seed. The seed might be in a nut, a fruit, a cone, or perhaps, attached to a propeller blown around by the wind. Different tree species make different types of seeds.

Boreal trees, such as conifers, make seeds on the ends of scales that are packed together in cones. The cones fall and shed the seeds when they ripen, which normally takes two or three years. An exception is the ancient sequoia tree of the temperate rain forest. It may keep its huge cones for up to twenty years before they drop.

Time to Sprout

Once a tree seed sprouts, it must try to grow on the forest floor, which is difficult because the large trees overhead block out the light. The best chance is to sprout in a space made by a fallen tree.

In the temperate rain forest, saplings sometimes sprout and grow on "nurse logs." These are fallen trees that soon start to rot because the atmosphere is so damp. Mosses, lichens, and ferns quickly cover the damp log and help it rot, making it a nutritious place for a seedling to live. Gradually, as the tree grows bigger, it throws out roots around the nurse log. Some temperate rain forest trees look like they are standing on stilts because the nurse logs they grew on have long since rotted, leaving a gap between the new trees' roots and the ground.

ROOTS GOING UP

In the last decade, scientists have started studying the temperate rain forests of the northwestern United States in greater detail. They use ropes and harnesses, and even cranes, to climb into trees as high as skyscrapers. Up in the greenery, they have found some surprising facts about the lives of trees.

When scientists climbed big-leaf maples in Olympic National Park, Washington, for example, they discovered thick bundles of mosses and lichens that gradually rotted to form piles of soil high up in the trees' nooks and crannies. They also found that the trees sent some of their own roots upward to collect nutrients from these soil piles.

Inside a Tree

A tree is made up of layers of different cells that do different jobs. A layer called the vascular cambium grows a new section of wood every year, which shows up as a tree ring on cut wood. You can count the rings on a tree log to see how old it is. At the very center of the tree is its oldest, hardest wood, called the heartwood.

Other layers of tree cells transport water, sap, or resin around the tree. Sap is a sugary solution that helps a tree grow. Maple syrup is made from the delicious sap of northern forest maples.

Resin is made by conifers and some deciduous trees. It is sticky, like molasses, and contains powerful chemicals. If a tree is damaged, its resin oozes out and hardens to heal the wound.

The outer bark wraps around the tree to protect it. Some trees, such as birch, have thin, papery bark. Others have thick, rough bark. The bark of the giant sequoia is so thick and spongy that it is virtually fireproof, so the tree can survive forest fires.

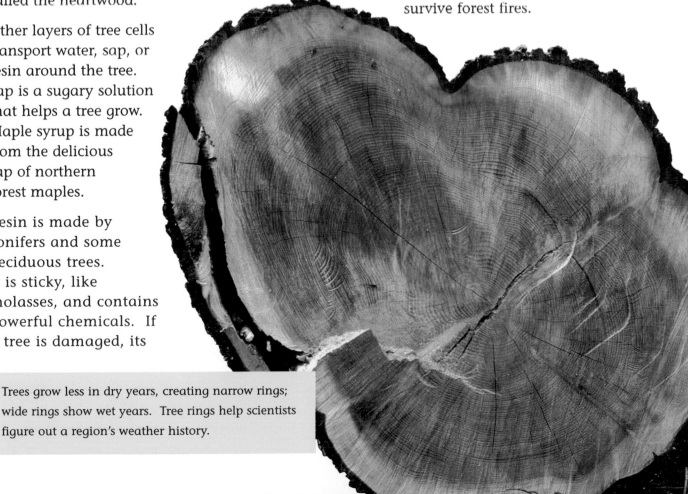

Trees grow less in dry years, creating narrow rings; wide rings show wet years. Tree rings help scientists figure out a region's weather history.

Forest Animals

Forests and woodlands are rich in animal life. The animals get their food from eating plants or by hunting other creatures. In winter, the animals have a variety of ways to deal with the cold.

Connections of Life

The well-being of all animals and plants in the forest is closely interconnected. For example, the carnivores (meat eaters), such as hawks and wolves, can survive only by eating smaller animals. Those creatures may, in turn, survive only by eating plants. The plants may be able to grow only because insects help pollinate them.

If trees die, or water or soil becomes polluted, plants and animals can be badly affected. Because of all the interconnections among forest life, the death of one plant or animal species can have far-reaching effects on all life in the forest.

Mammals

The large forest mammals include herbivores, such as moose and white-tailed deer, which eat only plants, and omnivores, such as bears, which will eat both plants and meat. Forest carnivores, such as grey wolves, lynx, and mountain lions, eat only meat, hunting other creatures, especially small mammals, for their food.

Some large mammals, such as this grizzly bear in Alaska, are skilled at catching fish in fast-flowing rivers and streams.

Some mammals migrate when winter comes, in order to find a warmer climate and a better food supply. A few species stay and brave the cold. Others go into a long winter sleep called hibernation, which enables them to survive the harsh weather.

Mammals are among the most endangered creatures in the forest because their food supply dwindles as deforestation continues to increase. Carnivores, such as mountain lions, are becoming much rarer and also more dangerous. When they cannot find food in the forest, they sometimes stray into human communities to search for food.

Birds

A wide range of birds feeds and nests in forests in spring and summer. The largest examples of forest birds are the eagles, and the largest among these are the bald eagle and the golden eagle, which average 30 to 35 inches (76 to 89 centimeters) long. The bald eagle's wingspan is about 7 feet (2 m).

In autumn, many forest birds migrate south to warmer places to find food. The berries, seeds, and small creatures they eat are not available in a harsh winter climate.

Water Creatures

The many streams, lakes, and bogs of forest lands make good homes for frogs, salamanders, and turtles. The lakes and rivers are rich in fish such as trout, perch, pike, and salmon.

Fish do not hibernate. Instead, they swim to waters that are too deep to freeze. Their body processes slow down in the cold waters so they can survive winter with less food.

Insects and Tiny Animals

In spring and summer, forests hum with insects. Clouds of flies and mosquitoes fill the air, providing plenty of meals for birds and small animals.

On the ground, especially in woodlands, there are lots of crawling creatures, such as beetles and earwigs, plus millions of tiny creatures too small to see without a microscope. One handful of woodland soil may contain up to 700 million organisms.

Most insects die in winter, leaving behind eggs that will hatch in spring. Meanwhile, worms survive the cold by burrowing deep beneath the frozen top layer of the soil to find warmer soil.

HIBERNATION

Hibernating means going into a deep sleep. In the Northern Hemisphere, mammals such as bears, bats, and gophers do this in November, waking up in about March, when the weather starts to get warm again. To prepare for winter, they eat a lot of food to give themselves a store of fat. Then, they hide somewhere sheltered, such as in a cave. As they sleep, their body temperature falls, their heartbeat and breathing slow down, and they live off their body fat. Hibernating animals' bodies are able to stay alive because they are not active in this resting state.

Natural Tree Enemies

Trees have some natural enemies that can damage and eventually kill them. Their worst enemies, however, have been accidentally introduced to forest areas by humans. Scientists must find ways to limit the damage.

Insect Attack

Tree pests include caterpillars that eat leaves and wood-boring beetles that burrow into wood to lay eggs. When beetle eggs hatch, the larvae eat out tunnels under the bark and eventually chew their way to the surface. Although the insects themselves don't kill the tree, they make openings for fungi to get under the tree bark. Some fungi can stop a tree from getting the nutrients and water it needs, eventually killing it.

Normally, tree-attacking insects do not kill whole forests. In fact, they help get rid of unhealthy or old trees, which are more easily attacked. That leaves room for younger, healthier ones to grow. Generally, natural pests are part of the balance of nature in a local area, but when humans introduce new pests, unnatural devastation can follow.

The Chestnut Blight Disaster

Once 4,000 million majestic chestnut trees covered the eastern United States. They were prized for their wood and their sweet nuts. Then, in 1904, a deadly fungus called chestnut blight was accidentally introduced into the country when some Asian chestnut trees were brought over and cultivated for their larger nuts. The U.S. trees were not naturally immune to the fungus, and, over the next few decades, 3,500 million chestnut trees died.

Tree scientists had to find some way to stop the devastation. They discovered a harmless form of the fungus that, when injected into a tree, stops the spread of the deadly form. They also started crossing different types of chestnut trees to breed new U.S. chestnut species that were immune to the fungus.

Work on tree and other plant diseases is called plant pathology. Like scientists working in human medicine, plant pathologists try to find out why diseases are occurring and how to cure them.

Dutch Elm Devastation

The Dutch elm fungus probably originated from the Himalayas in India, on crates made of infected wood. It is passed on by the elm bark beetle. This fungus caused the destruction of millions of elm trees in Europe and the United States during the twentieth century.

Scientists at the University of Toronto studied the problem and found that elms have a natural defense system against most diseases, which could be boosted by a tree injection called an elicitor. The elicitor helps the tree grow thicker walls around its cells, keeping out the fungus and preventing its spread.

The Wrong Wildlife

When new wildlife is introduced to an area by humans, it can have a harmful effect on forests. For instance, when gray squirrels were introduced to British forests from the United States, no one realized they would be so successful that they would drive out

14

the harmless local red squirrels. The gray squirrels cause much damage by eating tree bark, crops, bird eggs, and even, on occasion, small birds. Nowadays, we know much more about the potentially disastrous effect of changing a natural environment, and much more effort is being made to stop non-native animals and plants from spreading to new areas where they might cause problems.

This row of elm trees, killed by Dutch elm fungus, shows the destructive power of blights and diseases.

Acid Attack

These trees in the Harz Mountains of Germany have been badly damaged by acid rain.

In the past century, a new danger has started threatening the forests. Acid rain, a potential tree killer, is being caused by pollution from factories, power plants, and car exhausts.

Making Acid Rain

When fuels such as coal and oil burn, they make chemicals that rise into the air. Two of these chemicals — sulphur dioxide and nitrogen oxide — cause acid rain. Up in the atmosphere, they mix with water. Then sunlight helps turn the mixture into sulfuric acid and nitric acid. These environmentally harmful substances fall to earth in rain, snow, or fog. Acid rain is particularly bad in forests on high mountains that get lots of fog.

Wind can blow the acid pollution far from the place where it was first made. It may even end up falling in a different country. Some acid rain pollution is made naturally, for example, by volcanoes that erupt or by forest fires. Most of it, however, is made by industry and car exhaust fumes.

Not all acid pollution falls as rain. Some of it falls straight to the ground as tiny particles, poisoning the soil. Soil affected in this way has an unusually high amount of metals, such as aluminum and lead.

Scientists measure acid and its opposite, alkali, using a pH scale of numbers. The lower the number, the more acid there is. Ordinary rain has a pH of 5.5. Rain below pH 5 is regarded as damaging acid rain.

The Effect on Forests

Acid rain takes away important minerals from tree leaves and from the soil. It can block the tiny pores on leaves and stop them from working properly. Meanwhile, the toxic metals acid rain releases into the soil damage a tree's roots. Trees affected this way weaken and stop growing properly. Eventually, they may die.

Acid rain also falls into forest lakes and streams. Animals drink the polluted water and eat the pollution particles in plant life so that harmful metals begin to build up in their bodies, damaging their health and eventually making them infertile.

Tiny forest plants called lichens are a good indicator of the level of acid rain pollution in an area because the rain kills them quickly. In a place affected by acid rain, lichens soon disappear.

DEAD LAKES

A forest lake affected by acid rain looks very clear and clean. That's because all the tiny plankton and plants in the water have died. It may look clean, but it is lifeless.

Healthy forest lakes have a pH measurement of about 6.5 and support all kinds of creatures and plants. Once the pH drops below 6, everything alive begins to die.

In the heavily forested country of Sweden, there are about 90,000 lakes; over half of them have been polluted by acid rain. In the United States, it is estimated that one in five lakes has this problem. Another danger to forest water is effluent, which is liquid waste pumped into rivers by local industries. Fish stocks such as salmon are badly affected by effluents.

Finding Out the Facts

Mapping Pollution

Around the world, there are monitoring stations fitted with equipment to measure acid rain and particle pollution. Filters at the sites gather particles from the air, and the amounts in the filters are checked by chemists. Chemists also gather samples from planes sent over forests and from equipment set up on high forest platforms.

Now, pollution is monitored from space, too. Satellites use sensing equipment to collect data on the atmosphere. For example, satellite sensors can measure the atmosphere for levels of carbon monoxide, a polluting gas produced by cars.

Scientists have developed computer programs that use all this data to build virtual models, or maps, of Earth's atmosphere and landscape. These maps can show where the pollution is coming from and where it is likely to move next.

On the ground, forest experts keep a close eye on the state of trees and take soil, air, and water samples to analyze. By studying soil samples, scientists have discovered that rich, thick soil is much better at coping with acid rain than thin, crumbly soil, which is one reason why the effects of pollution vary from place to place.

Animal Indicators

Animal experts study forest creatures, recording their population rates, diets, and ways of life. They have found that when the biggest forest creatures, the carnivores, start dying out, it is often a sign of health difficulties all the way down the food chain.

One example of noting health concerns and acting on them is the work done on ospreys and bald eagles in the Great Lakes region of North America. Experts discovered that the birds were not breeding successfully. It turned out that many of their eggshells were so weak that they broke before the chicks could hatch. Breakage was due to toxic chemicals in the fish the birds were eating. Some pesticides were pinpointed as problems, and their use was limited by law.

GLOBAL WARMING

The phrase "global warming" means the warming up of Earth's atmosphere. Scientific data appears to show that it is happening and could be due to pollution. Carbon dioxide gas, released when wood, coal, or oil burns, is increasing in the atmosphere and could be blanketing Earth so that less heat escapes into space. Forests use vast amounts of CO_2 in photosynthesis (*see page 8*), and trees store huge amounts of carbon in their wood. What would happen if the forests died, ending their photosynthesis and releasing huge amounts of CO_2 when they were burned? Clearly, the oxygen that forests — "the lungs of the world" — produce would be greatly reduced, and life that relies on oxygen would suffer. The total effects remain unknown, and the subject of global warming continues to cause heated debates among conservationists, industries, and even countries around the world.

Since the use of certain types of agricultural pesticides in the Great Lakes area of North America has been reduced, the populations of osprey and bald eagles (*shown here*) have started to recover.

19

Fighting Back for Forests

The middle of a busy city or an industrial factory complex may seem a long way from a quiet forest glade, but what happens in these highly developed places affects the forests a great deal because pollution is blown long distances by the wind. Here are a few of the answers that scientists have come up with to limit forest damage.

Factory Clean-Up

Most acid rain gases come from factories, power stations, and oil refineries. These gases can be greatly reduced by adding new equipment that absorbs gas emissions. For example, sulfur gas can be absorbed by a slurry of calcium hydroxide injected into a factory chimney. Similarly, pulp and paper mills, which are often found in forest areas, can be fitted with treatment machinery so that their liquid waste (called effluent) can be made nontoxic before it is washed into nearby rivers.

Industrial clean-up inventions have led to a drop in pollution in many areas in the last few years. Clean-up adds cost to businesses, however, so not all companies around the world are happy or willing to do it.

Factories and power stations, such as this one near Hong Kong, can be fitted with equipment to help reduce the amount of pollution they make.

LAND OF THE SPOTTED OWL

The northern spotted owl lives in areas of old-growth conifer forests in the Pacific northwest of the United States and Canada. Old-growth refers to forests that have never been cut down and replanted. In the early 1990s, logging was halted in seventeen U.S. National Forest Parks to protect the northern spotted owls.

Conservationists were delighted, but loggers were furious. They could not agree on which was more important — protecting creatures or protecting income that comes from jobs. Conservationists argue that we must try to keep biodiversity, preserving as many animal and plant species as possible in order to keep Earth healthy. They also argue that it is impossible to put a price on health and that protecting forests helps protect people — and their jobs — in the long run. Either way, conservation is still a hot political issue in many countries.

Cleaning up Cars

Car exhaust fumes are full of poisonous gases. Therefore, cars are now fitted with catalytic converters, chambers in the exhaust systems that alter the gases and make them much less harmful. Environmentalists hope that alternative fuels will provide cleaner transportation. Nonpolluting electric cars, hybrid cars that use both gas and electricity, and cars that use hydrogen and oxygen may become more popular. Scientists have even invented cars powered by sunlight or vegetable oil.

Changing Laws

Acid rain pollution is an issue for the whole world because one country's industrial pollution can harm another country's forests. International laws have been passed to try to limit poisonous gas pollution. Some countries, however, refuse to sign these legal agreements because they think these laws might damage the profits of their industries and cost people their jobs.

Saving Lakes

Acidity in lakes can be controlled by adding large amounts of lime to the water. Lime is a harmless alkaline, the opposite type of substance to acid. It can be pumped into a river or lake, but its effects do not last forever. It has to be added every few years to help the water support life.

Increased car usage leads to more acid rain.

Using Forests

Wood from forests is used in many different ways in our homes and in industry, too. Electricity can come from forest hydroelectric projects, and some forest areas have oil resources. The effect of all this industry on forests and on local people is very controversial. Many businesses, governments, and conservationists argue bitterly over industry's impact.

Forest Industry

Forest products include furniture, building materials of all kinds, paper, and fuel logs. Industrial timber companies practice clear-cutting, which means cutting down wide areas of forest in one large operation. The timber companies that do this are strongly encouraged to replant the trees. Called "sustainable" forestry, this practice cannot replace virgin or old-growth forests, but it can protect forest lands, and it is increasing in such large areas as North America and Northern Europe. Many conservationists fear that, in more remote, isolated places, such as the Russian taiga, companies could do great damage to forests by clear-cutting vast areas without replanting.

Some conservationists would prefer to preserve the wilderness untouched, but the world demand for wood is skyrocketing, so conservationists and businesses are trying to work together to regenerate forests. The best forest businesses do all they can to renew the forests they use, recycle their waste, and make sure they are not polluting local water supplies. These good ecology practices, however, do not happen all over the world.

A clear-cut area, where all the trees have been cut down, destroys animal homes.

FIRST NATIONS

Although the boreal forest has a small population, many of its people have long histories and unique cultures. In Canada, there are many First Nations reservations in forested areas. The people of these tribes traditionally rely on the forest to make a living, doing their own logging and wood product-making. They battle to save the forest from large-scale industrial damage and pollution. Without the forest, they know their way of life, in harmony with the forest, would disappear.

In Europe, the Sami people in northern Scandinavia make their living from herding reindeer, but their rights to herd through the boreal forest are being challenged by private forest owners.

Meanwhile, in the far eastern area of Russia, ancient tribes such as the Koryak people are fast disappearing as their way of life dies out. They have found they have no rights over the forest that their ancestors once cared for.

Problems with Plantations

Sometimes logging companies cut down old-growth forests, usually a mix of different trees, and replant a commercial plantation with only one fast-growing conifer species in it. Conifer plantations with just one type of tree support far fewer plants and animals than a mix of trees. Therefore, much of the original animal and plant life disappear forever. Conservationists encourage companies to replant using a mix, to try to help preserve wildlife.

Non-wood Industries

The industries that damage forests the most are the ones that do not replace the trees they clear. Oil extraction, mining, road-building, hydroelectric dams, clearing the land for farming and new communities all destroy trees forever. If planned badly, these projects can cause serious damage and pollution of the water supplies in the local areas. On the other hand, these activities bring jobs and money to northern forest countries, which is good in the short term.

Logging brings jobs and money to forest areas.

Managing a Forest

Foresters try to look after forested areas so that they stay healthy and productive. The science of managing a woodland is called silviculture.

When to Cut

A forest that is overcrowded can become unhealthy. Therefore, foresters need to cut down diseased trees to stop problems from spreading, and they sometimes need to thin out forests, cutting down some of the tallest, oldest trees to give the younger, shorter trees more light to help them grow.

Many birds, such as these woodpeckers, eat forest insects, including harmful pests.

It is a good idea, however, to leave a few dead tree skeletons in a forest. These are called snags, and they make good nesting homes for useful birds such as woodpeckers, which help keep the forest healthy by eating insect pests.

Clear-Cutting Properly

Large, ill-planned clear-cutting can lead to soil being eroded, local water supplies being polluted, and wildlife being destroyed. Carefully planned clear-cutting can avoid these problems. Loggers can, for example, leave strips of untouched forest, called buffer strips, between their clear-cuts to encourage wildlife and protect streams.

Clear-cutting leaves a landscape looking bare and scarred, and makes forest animals homeless, but the forest will gradually regrow through natural seeding and replanting. It takes about twenty years for a clear-cut forest to regenerate completely.

Forest Fires

For many years, as a safety measure in the forests of the United States, all forest fires were put out. Gradually, the forest under-growth grew thicker and the trees became overcrowded, eventually, causing fires to rage much more uncontrollably whenever they accidentally broke out.

Now, foresters understand that carefully controlled fires are good for forests. Fires help clear out dead undergrowth, and they even help some seeds grow. Nowadays, foresters are allowed to start fires deliberately in forests that need clearing. First, however, they chemically treat undergrowth and dig ditches around the planned fire area. The ditches stop the fire from spreading, and the treatment of the undergrowth helps prevent the fire from flaring up too much.

Unplanned forest fires can be started by lightning strikes or by careless human behavior, such as lighting campfires during dry weather or a drought. When accidental fires threaten human safety, teams of firefighters sometimes go into the fire area by helicopter. Smoke-jumpers, who are highly trained forest firefighters, parachute down to try to stop the fire. Planes may also be sent in to "bomb" the fire with water.

Forests Make Money

People love to visit forests. In fact, forest tourism makes much more money than timber logging. Millions of people visit the National Forest parks in the United States every year and generate hundreds of millions of dollars for the U.S. economy.

Forest managers must plan paths for the visitors, safely away from dangers such as rockfalls or breeding wild bears. Visitors need facilities, too, such as parking places, campsites, and information centers where they can learn about the forest and the creatures that live there.

People love to go for walks through woodlands. Clearly marked paths help protect fragile plants.

Watching the Forest

It is important for scientists to study and map the world's forests. That way, it is easier to keep track of dangers, such as fires, the effects of pollution, and illegal logging, and also to figure out how best to keep these vast areas of Earth healthy.

Mapping with Satellites

GPS (Global Positioning System) has made mapping remote forest areas easier. GPS consists of twenty-seven satellites orbiting Earth. At any time, anywhere on Earth, someone with a GPS receiver can locate four of these satellites. The receiver measures its distance from each satellite and uses the data to figure out its own position on the ground. In a remote forest, GPS is vital to keep people from becoming lost and for recording the position of geographical features, such as hills and rivers.

Computer Pictures

Forest-watching is made a lot easier by computers, which can store all kinds of data and convert numerical information into three-dimensional (3 D) pictures.

A computer GIS (Geographical Information System) can be used to create a range of 3 D maps, showing, for example, different kinds of trees, forest fires and burned areas,

This satellite image shows a forest fire in progress in Montana.

places where erosion is happening, or local streams and rivers.

Computer programs of this kind can even be made to predict future events, using the data they have to create maps of what is likely to happen. They might be used to help predict forest growth, the rate of soil erosion, or flooding.

Watching from Above

Sensors on planes and satellites can be used to build up pictures of the land below. For example, airborne radar can be used to plot the shape of the land, and a satellite image can show different forest features in great detail. Sensors might show an area where trees are being cut down illegally.

Predicting Fires

Forest experts try to predict forest fires by measuring the moisture in the ground and in firewood logs. If there is a lot of moisture, there is less likelihood of fire. In times of drought, moisture dries out and fire becomes much more likely.

The greenness of a forest is one good indicator of fire risk. When forests start to dry out, they lose their greenness.

Up a tree: This scientist captures insects in a net to study later in a laboratory.

KEEPING WATCH ON CRITTERS

Forest biologists study insect wildlife in a forest by climbing the trees and using nets to trap specimens. Back on the ground, they take a look at what they have caught. Using this method, hundreds of new insect species have been discovered. By recording these species and keeping an eye on whether their numbers rise or fall, biologists may get an early warning of problems that might affect forest health. For example, they might discover an insect-borne blight, such as Dutch elm fungus, or an unhealthy increase in gypsy moths.

What Can You Do?

Here are some suggestions for ways that you can find out more about forests and help stop their destruction.

Watch What You Buy

Whenever possible, try to encourage your family to buy wood that has been cut from a sustainable forest that is properly managed to preserve and renew the environment. This type of wood has a forest certificate mark on its packaging, which means the forest it has come from has been independently checked for good forestry. By supporting good forestry, you will be helping maintain both forest communities and the environment.

Recycle Your Stuff

Try to use recycled paper when you can, and make sure you recycle the paper that you no longer need. In the long run, it will help reduce the number of trees cut down. Find out about recycling programs in your area and use them to recycle your trash.

Be Energy-Efficient

Make sure you do not waste energy such as electricity. The less power you use, the less you contribute to global warming.

You can also help by cutting out nonessential car rides. Maybe you could ride your bike more, or start a ride-sharing plan with your friends when you go to school or on trips.

Be a Good Visitor

When you visit woodlands or forests, make sure you do not damage plants, harm animals, or do something that might start a fire.

If you go to woodlands or forests for a picnic, make sure you take away your trash afterwards.

Adopt a Tree

All over the world, there are adopt-a-tree programs that you can join to help fund conservation work. Ask your teacher to help you find one near where you live. You can adopt trees for other people, too, which makes an unusual gift.

Get Involved

Find out if there are programs you can get involved in to help care for and monitor your local woods. Ask your teacher to help your class find ways to contribute and help.

On the Web

Here are some useful web site addresses relating to woodlands and forests:

www.blueplanetbiomes.org/deciduous_forest.htm
Find out more about Earth's deciduous forests, including the plants, animals, and climates of these unique biomes, and explore links to related sites.

www.borealforest.org
Discover the world of boreal forests through this site based on the forests of Northwest Canada.

www.familyfun.go.com
Here are some practical, fun ideas for things to do the next time you visit a woodland. Type the word "woods" into the site search area to find a list of ideas. Try figuring out the age of a tree — and even listening to a tree.

www.nationalgeographic.com/kids/
Learn about world habitats, play games, try activities, and get homework help, maps, and more by clicking on icons and subject headings on this site.

www.panda.org
Find out about the World Wildlife Fund and its strong conservation work around the world, including work on the northern forests.

www.tappi.org/paperu
Go to "paper university" to find out how paper products are made from wood and to play paper-related games.

www.yahooligans.yahoo.com
Once you get to this site, go to "science and nature," then click on "living things," then "botany," and, finally, "trees" to get a long list of tree-related, user-friendly sites that you can explore.

Glossary

acid rain
moisture containing harmful chemicals, which falls to Earth as rain, snow, or fog

bark
a tree's outer protective layer

biodiversity
the wide genetic variety of living things on Earth; providing essential options for life, food, and medicines

biome
a very large habitat where living conditions are ecologically connected and broadly similar across a wide area, such as an ocean biome or a desert biome

boreal forest
the giant evergreen forest in the upper part of the Northern Hemisphere

broad-leaved trees
trees with wide, flat leaves

carbon dioxide (CO$_2$)
a gas released when wood, coal, or oil burns

carnivores
animals that only eat meat

catalytic converter
equipment in the exhaust system of a car that makes exhaust fumes less polluting

chlorophyll
a green chemical found in plant leaves

clear-cutting
cutting down all the trees in an area

cone
the woody, scaly fruit of a pine or fir tree; on the end of each scale is a seed, such as a pine nut

deciduous trees
trees that lose their leaves in winter

deforestation
the destruction of trees over large areas

epiphytes
plants that grow on other plants and dangle their roots in the air to get the moisture they need

erosion
the process by which soil is worn away by wind, water, or other natural forces

evergreen trees
trees that do not lose their leaves in winter

First Nations
communities of people who have lived in the boreal forest over centuries

fungi
small plants that do not photosynthesize but instead get the food they need from dead leaves and rotting bark

GIS
(Geographical Information System) a computer program for creating 3 D maps

heartwood
the oldest, hardest layer of wood, found in the center of a tree

herbivores
animals that eat only plants

hibernation
the process of sleeping through the winter

lichens
tiny plants that grow on bark or stone

migrate
to travel to new areas to find food. Many northern forest animals migrate south in winter.

Northern Hemisphere
the northern half of the world

nurse log
a fallen log that provides an ideal place for a new tree seedling to grow

old-growth forests
forests that have never been harvested and regrown

omnivores
animals that eat meat and plants

oxygen (O_2)
a gas, essential to human respiration, which is produced by trees during photosynthesis

pH scale
a way to measure the amount of acid in a liquid, such as in acid rain or lakes

photosynthesis
the process by which green plants take in sunlight, CO_2, and water to make oxygen and food for themselves and the animals that eat them

plant pathology
the study of tree and other plant diseases

resin
a sticky substance made by a tree to help heal damage to its bark

sap
a sugary solution that circulates and carries nutrients throughout a tree

silviculture
the science of developing and managing forests to keep them healthy and in balance

smoke-jumpers
highly trained forest firefighters who parachute into threatened forest areas to try to stop fire from spreading

snags
dead tree skeletons still standing in a forest

taiga
the name given to the huge area of the subarctic boreal forest that grows in Russia

temperate weather
mild, wet climate conditions found in both the Northern and Southern Hemispheres

temperate rain forest
a rain forest that grows in a part of the world where there are cool as well as warm seasons

tree ring
a tree's yearly growth of new wood, forming a ring in the tree's trunk. The rings can be counted as one year per ring to show a tree's age.

Index